GARDENER'S
BOOK OF
HANDMADE
GIFTS

A GARDENER'S BOOK OF HANDMADE GIFTS

HOW TO GROW AND MAKE DELIGHTFUL PRESENTS FOR
AND FROM THE GARDEN: 20 CHARMING PRACTICAL IDEAS
SHOWN IN 120 STUNNING, EVOCATIVE PHOTOGRAPHS

Stephanie Donaldson

LORENZ BOOKS

This edition is published by Lorenz Books, an imprint of Anness Publishing Ltd,
Hermes House, 88–89 Blackfriars Road, London SE1 8HA; tel. 020 7401 2077; fax 020 7633 9499
www.lorenzbooks.com; www.annesspublishing.com

If you like the images in this book and would like to investigate using them for publishing, promotions
or advertising, please visit our website www.practicalpictures.com for more information.

UK agent: The Manning Partnership Ltd; tel. 01225 478444; fax 01225 478440; sales@manning-partnership.co.uk
UK distributor: Grantham Book Services Ltd; tel. 01476 541080; fax 01476 541061; orders@gbs.tbs-ltd.co.uk
North American agent/distributor: National Book Network; tel. 301 459 3366; fax 301 429 5746; www.nbnbooks.com
Australian agent/distributor: Pan Macmillan Australia; tel. 1300 135 113;
fax 1300 135 103; customer.service@macmillan.com.au
New Zealand agent/distributor: David Bateman Ltd; tel. (09) 415 7664; fax (09) 415 8892

Publisher: Joanna Lorenz
Senior Editor: Lindsay Porter
Assistant Editor: Emma Gray
Reader: Joy Wotton
Designer: Nigel Partridge
Photographer: Michelle Garrett
Stylists: Michelle Garrett and Stephanie Donaldson
Production Controller: Ben Worley

ETHICAL TRADING POLICY

Because of our ongoing ecological investment programme, you, as our customer, can have the pleasure and
reassurance of knowing that a tree is being cultivated on your behalf to naturally replace the materials used to
make the book you are holding. For further information about this scheme, go to www.annesspublishing.com/trees

A CIP catalogue record for this book is available from the British Library.

Previously published as *Gifts From the Garden*

Contents

Introduction	6	Vegetable Sacks	36
Gifts for the Gardener	8	Weathered Garden Furniture	38
New Gardener's Gift Set	10	Customized Nesting Box	40
Gardener's Hand-care Kit	12	Wind Chimes	42
Gardener's Apron	14	Natural Garden Gifts	44
Gardener's Scarf	16	Tribute to Monet	46
Decorated Rubber Boots	18	Topiary Herbs	48
Decorated Hand Tools	20	The Language of Flowers	50
Provençal Watering Can	22	Lavender Bottles	52
Gardener's Storage Box	24	Blooming Borage	54
Gifts for the Garden	26	Grow your own Wine Kit	56
Herald of Spring	28	Bouquet Garni	58
Seed Packets	30	Sage and Tansy Heart	60
Decoupage Seed Storage Box	32	Templates	62
Row Markers	34	Index	64

INTRODUCTION

·· ☙ ··

We have been gardeners since Adam and Eve cultivated Eden, and even if gardening is now a leisure activity more often than a necessity, the instinct to till and sow remains deep within us. For many of us, our garden is our only real connection with the uncontrollable natural world – with the vagaries of climate, the variability of soil, the vigour of weeds and the voracity of pests.

While the garden holds as many disappointments as delights, every gardener is always full of hopeful

dreams. The seeds we sow flourish in our imagination, and bulbs pierce the soil like well-rehearsed synchronized swimmers, with never a shoot too premature or tardy. Of course we know differently, but each year we entertain the possibility that maybe this year will be the one when our dreams come true.

Gardening's combination of activity and contemplation means that it can very often be enjoyed in solitude: even when a garden is jointly cultivated, there is a tendency towards a companionable hierarchy, with helpers deferring to the expertise and vision of the "head" gardener. However, although dedicated gardeners can be territorial, they are invariably generous in their desire to share the results of their efforts. If you love your garden, there is nothing more satisfying than exchanging ideas and discoveries, seeds and cuttings with fellow enthusiasts. Gifts of plants and produce from your own plot will not fail to delight your gardening friends and will be a joy to give because they represent your mutual passion.

Best of all, the bounty of your garden may inspire others to take up their trowels and forks for the first time: a bag of your home-grown vegetables, a selection of spring bulbs, or a gift of gardening tools that you know from experience will serve them well, may be the spur a new gardener needs to get going.

There is a whole world of creative possibilities in

LEFT: Painting a watering can protects it from the weather and makes a charming, aesthetically pleasing gift.

ABOVE: *The typical gardener's retreat is packed with old but useful implements that can be turned into delightful gifts.*

all aspects of gardening, and the projects in this book have been inspired by a love of gardening and many happy hours spent pottering in a shed, conservatory or kitchen. The useful and decorative accessories celebrate the importance of gardening in our lives and enhance the pleasure of this enduring occupation. Rewarding to make and to give, they are designed to be used in the garden or potting shed, or to restore and delight the tired gardener at the end of a satisfying day. All of them are original, thoughtful gifts to be enjoyed by anyone who loves their garden.

GIFTS FOR THE GARDENER

· · ❦ · ·

*F*rom beautifully decorated tools to delicately scented
hand lotion – here are perfect gift ideas for gardeners.

NEW GARDENER'S GIFT SET

Long experience teaches the gardener which tools are absolutely essential. These are the ones that seldom become rusty and, if they do, must be renovated or replaced, while less useful tools languish at the back of the shed, too complicated to use or too difficult to clean. The selection of tools in this gift set has been made from experience and would be very useful to a new gardener. It would, perhaps, be ideal as a house-warming present for a young couple about to tackle their first garden or as an appealing retirement gift for someone who has never previously had the time to garden.

Materials and Equipment
25 cm (10 in) terracotta pot
shredded wood or straw for packing
trowel
fork
dibber
weed lifter (optional)
secateurs
string
gloves
sisal string
label

1 Fill the pot with shredded wood or straw. Pack it tightly to ensure it will keep the tools upright.

2 Push the tools into the packing material so that they stand upright and give the appearance that they are growing out of the pot. Add more packing material if necessary.

ABOVE: *Gardeners' favourite tools are used time and again, and are always kept close to hand.*

3 For the finishing touch, tie a long piece of sisal string twice around the terracotta pot and add a label to identify the giver.

BELOW: *New gardeners can look forward to enjoying their own produce.*

GARDENER'S HAND-CARE KIT

· · ~ · ·

Working in the garden is wonderfully therapeutic and excellent exercise, but your hands can suffer, especially in cold or wet weather. This natural, healing barrier cream can be used to protect the hands when applied before gardening and as a treatment for chapped hands or cuts and scratches. The camomile oil is soothing and excellent for chilblains, while the geranium oil helps wounds and scratches to heal quickly, controls inflammation and improves circulation and skin tone. The lemon oil softens hardened skin. Pack the cream in a box with a bar of soap, an absorbent towel, a pumice stone and a nail-brush, and the gardener will find everything needed to keep hands in tiptop condition.

Materials and Equipment
25 g (1 oz) lanolin
15 g (1/2 oz) white beeswax
double boiler and whisk
75 g (3 oz) almond oil
50 ml (2 fl oz, 1/4 cup) purified water
10 drops camomile oil
5 drops geranium oil
5 drops lemon oil
ceramic lidded container
wooden box
selection of hand-care items

1 Slowly melt the lanolin and beeswax in a double boiler. Whisk the mixture, gradually adding the almond oil. The mixture will thicken slightly and become opaque.

2 Still whisking, add the water a few drops at a time. The mixture will very quickly emulsify into a thick cream.

3 Stir in the essential oils and pour into a lidded container. Pack the container in a wooden box with a selection of hand-care items.

LEFT: *The home-made hand cream makes a very welcome gift when presented in a decorative pot along with other cleansing treats.*

GARDENER'S APRON

· · 🙠 · ·

If you are the sort of gardener who likes to nip out into the garden for ten minutes or so, in between other tasks, then this gardener's apron will prove an ideal garment. Everything can be kept at hand for a productive potter without wasting precious minutes locating gloves, secateurs, scissors, string or raffia. The apron can be made from scratch or the "flower-pot" pockets and brass rings can be added to a ready-made apron. Either way, you will be ready to garden at a moment's notice.

Materials and Equipment

TO MAKE FROM SCRATCH:
old apron
newspaper and pencil
1 m (1 yd) dark green sailcloth
scissors
dressmaker's pins
cotton thread: dark green and beige
sewing machine
5 m (5 yd) beige woven tape
tape measure
30 cm (12 in) natural hessian
needle
8 x 2.5 cm (1 in) brass rings
FOR A READY-MADE APRON:
newspaper and pencil
tape measure
30 cm (12 in) natural hessian
dressmaker's pins
scissors
sewing machine
beige cotton thread
3 m (3 yd) beige woven tape
needle
8 2.5 cm (1 in) brass rings

ABOVE: *The flowerpot pockets hold the gardener's essentials.*

1 Fold the old apron in half vertically, lay it on the newspaper and draw around it, adding a 1 cm (½ in) allowance. Cut out the pattern, pin it on to the sailcloth and cut around the pattern.

2 Hem around the apron with green cotton thread. Cut three 60 cm (24 in) lengths of tape. Using beige cotton thread, attach one length to go around the neck and the other two at each side at waist level.

3 Carefully cut out two paper patterns for the two sizes of pocket, following the templates at the back of the book. Pin them on the hessian, and cut out one small pocket and two large pockets.

4 Fold over a 2 cm (¾ in) seam allowance and pin in place. Zigzag stitch all around. Cut a piece of tape 19 cm (7½ in) long. Turn under and stitch 1 cm (½ in) at each end.

5 Pin the beige woven tape to the top edge of the small top pocket to make the "rim". It should overlap slightly at each end. Turn under a 1 cm (½ in) seam allowance and stitch in place.

6 Cut four 25 cm (10 in) lengths of tape. Pin two pieces of tape to the top edge of each of the large pockets to make the flowerpot rim. They should overlap slightly at each end. Turn under a 1 cm (½ in) seam allowance and stitch in place.

7 Cut eight 10 cm (4 in) lengths of tape. Thread a brass ring on to each piece, turn over 2 cm (¾ in) of tape and stitch to secure the ring.

8 Pin two taped rings to the rim of the small pocket and three taped rings to the large pockets, so they are just above the lower edge of the rim. Using the needle and thread, stitch close to the upper rim. Sew the pockets on to the apron.

GARDENER'S SCARF

· · ❧ · ·

Many a happy day's gardening has been ruined by the persistent presence of wasps, flies and midges. This colourful scarf has a little pocket that holds a sachet impregnated with essential oils with insect-repellent properties. Worn around the neck, it will help keep the buzzing and biting insects at bay. A variety of oils are suitable; although citronella is the best known, it is more pungent than aromatic, and you may prefer to use lavender or peppermint oil or a mixture of lemon and clove or geranium and eucalyptus. To complete the gift, a brightly coloured hessian bag can be made to hold the scarf along with a supply of sachets and a bottle of the essential oil, together with instructions for their use.

Materials and Equipment
fabric, 50 x 50 cm (20 x 20 in), plus
20 x 10 cm (8 x 4 in) for pocket
dressmaker's pins
iron
sewing machine
matching thread
needle
4 pieces felt, 15 x 7.5 cm (6 x 3 in)
cotton wool
or wadding
essential oil

1 Fold over a 1 cm (1/2 in) hem all around the fabric for the scarf. Pin in place, press with a hot iron and stitch the hem. Fold over a hem on one edge of the fabric for the pocket and stitch.

2 Fold the pocket in half, right sides together, pin the raw edges together and stitch. Turn the pocket right side out and press.

3 Pin the pocket on to one corner of the scarf and stitch in place.

4 Fold each felt piece in half and stuff with cotton wool or wadding impregnated with 6–10 drops of oil for each sachet. Pin around the edges and stitch securely.

LEFT: *Provide several of the oil-soaked sachets with the scarf.*

DECORATED RUBBER BOOTS

For those whose rubber boots are permanently caked in a thick layer of mud, the idea of decorating their boots may seem risible. For the less earnest gardener, this is an attractive way of personalizing and decorating utilitarian footwear. In households with stacks of boots at the back door, it also has the advantage of making your pair immediately apparent. An illustrated flora is a good source of botanical illustrations and, depending on your ability, you can either sketch them straight on to the boot or take a tracing. Enamel paints are available in small pots from art shops or DIY stores.

ABOVE: *A different design can be painted on each boot. Choose flower or vegetable motifs appropriate to the wearer.*

Materials and Equipment
rubber boots
soft pencil
felt-tip pen
enamel paints: yellow, green and white
small paintbrush

1 Trace or draw your chosen design on to the boots using a soft pencil. When the design is complete, draw over the outline with a felt-tip pen.

2 Paint the main areas of the design and leave to dry overnight.

3 Check that the painted area is fully dry, then paint the details.

4 Leave the enamel paint to dry for a minimum of three days before gift-wrapping the rubber boots.

DECORATED HAND TOOLS

Trowels and forks are easily mislaid in the border when the telephone rings, a friend arrives or something else distracts the gardener from the matter in hand. They frequently reappear some time later, generally long after they have been replaced by another earth-toned version, equally ambitious to lose itself as soon as possible. Evidently it is not in the interest of the manufacturers to make their tools more visible, as sales would fall dramatically, but brightly coloured handles decorated with children's insect stickers turn them into distinctive gifts that won't be overlooked.

2 Glue the stickers on to the handles and leave the glue to dry. If you are decorating the tools for someone who dislikes creepy-crawlies, use flower stickers instead.

Materials and Equipment
wooden-handled tools
fine-grade sandpaper
yellow gloss paint
paintbrushes
sheet of insect stickers
PVA glue
satin-finish varnish

ABOVE: *Plain hand tools may get lost in the garden. Bright paint and eye-catching motifs will make them easy to spot in the flowerbed.*

1 Rub down the wooden handles of the tools with fine-grade sandpaper. Paint the handles with two coats of gloss paint, leaving the paint to dry between coats.

3 Apply several coats of satin-finish varnish, leaving the handles to dry before applying the next coat.

PROVENÇAL WATERING CAN

• • 🙢 • •

There was a time when it appeared that the old-fashioned, galvanized, metal watering can would be permanently abandoned in favour of the lighter plastic alternative. Plastic cans are sadly lacking in style and cannot be left around the garden as decorative objects in their own right, whereas the classic metal can is both attractive and functional. Not long ago, old watering cans could be bought for next to nothing, but they have now become highly desirable collectables. A beautiful old can in good condition really needs no embellishment, but a traditionally shaped modern can is ripe for decoration.

Materials and Equipment
galvanized metal watering can
turquoise satin-finish oil-based paint
paintbrushes
craft knife
cutting mat or thick card
colouring pencils or crayons
PVA glue and brush
soft cloth
matt varnish

1 Paint the watering can with two coats of turquoise satin-finish oil-based paint. Leave to dry fully between coats.

2 Make four enlarged photocopies of the olive branch motif at the back of the book. Cut carefully round them with a craft knife, protecting the work surface with a cutting mat or thick card. Colour the leaves green and highlight the olives with a strong purple or dark blue.

ABOVE LEFT: *Despite its delicate appearance, the decoration on this can will last many years and withstand all but the roughest of treatments.*

3 Seal the coloured motifs by brushing on a mixture of one part PVA glue to two parts water. Leave on a non-absorbent surface to dry.

4 Coat the reverse of the motifs with undiluted PVA glue and position them around the top of the watering can. Use a soft cloth to wipe off any excess glue, but make sure that all the edges are firmly stuck down. The PVA will dry clear.

5 Protect the watering can with several layers of matt varnish, allowing the varnish to dry fully between coats. This will give a damage-resistant finish.

GARDENER'S STORAGE BOX

W ith the best will in the world, it is hard to keep all the little bits and pieces used in the garden under control. Here is a delightful idea that may make the task slightly easier. A small set of storage drawers is given a decorative finish, and then each drawer is "labelled" by stapling a sample of the contents on to the outside.

Materials and Equipment
unpainted set of storage drawers
blue-green wood varnish
paintbrush
coarse-grade sandpaper
sisal string
ruler
scissors
samples of vine-eyes, plant rings, etc.
staple gun and staples

1 Paint the front and sides of the boxes and the outer shell with varnish. Leave to dry thoroughly.

2 Rub down with sandpaper to give the box an aged effect, paying particular attention to the corners and edges.

3 Cut a 7.5 cm (3 in) length of string for each drawer.

4 Position the sample item on the front of the drawer and staple the string to the drawer in two places to hold it in position.

5 As the finishing touch, fray the ends of the string.

ABOVE: *A flat wooden tray can also be used to contain clutter.*

GIFTS FOR THE GARDEN

· · ❧ · ·

*I*nspirational projects for useful and decorative gifts to add
character to the potting shed and the garden using stencils,
decoupage, paint effects and wirework.

HERALD OF SPRING

· · ❧ · ·

Gardeners are always delighted to be given spring bulbs. Order them well ahead of time or get down to the garden centre early for the best possible choice. To make this a really special gift, the bulbs are removed from their plastic bags and packed instead into hessian bags. These allow the bulbs to breathe and can be used to store them after flowering. A new wooden box is "weathered" by painting it with diluted liquid seaweed plant food, and some terracotta pots complete the gift.

Materials and Equipment
3 pieces hessian, 60 x 45 cm
(24 x 18 in)
dressmaker's pins
sewing machine
matching cotton thread
3 bags of bulbs
scissors
stiff card
glue
hole punch
sisal string
wooden box, approximately
30 x 25 cm (12 x 10 in)
liquid seaweed plant food
paintbrush
3 terracotta pots
plant labels
bulb fibre (optional)

2 Select a picture from the packaging to use as the label. Cut round it and mount it on stiff card, then cut carefully around the image.

BELOW: *Decorative labels indicate the contents of the bag. Cultivation instructions may be written on the back.*

1 To make the sacks, fold each piece of hessian in half. Pin and stitch the side and base seams. Remove the bulbs from their original packaging and place them in the sacks.

3 To attach the label to the bag, punch a hole in it and thread through a length of sisal string. Fray the ends.

4 To "weather" the box, paint it with a mixture of one part seaweed plant food and one part water.

5 Fill the box with the sacks of bulbs and the pots. Plant labels and a bag of bulb fibre may also be added.

SEED PACKETS

· · 🙟 · ·

When a favourite plant sets seed, it is a pleasant gesture to collect some of the seeds and pass them on to friends as a gift. These colourful seed packets require a little forethought, but the results are so stunning that they are definitely worth the effort. Photographs of the flowers are mounted on an outline of the seed packet and then copied on a colour photocopier to produce the required number of packets for each flower. Provided you have taken the photographs of your plants looking their best and have saved the seeds, making the packets can be delayed until the dark winter months.

Materials and Equipment
sheets of A4 paper
pencil
15 x 10 cm (6 x 4 in) photographs
glue
cutting mat or thick card
craft knife or scissors
metal ruler
double-sided tape
seeds

1 Draw two seed packets on a sheet of A4 paper, enlarging the template at the back of the book.

2 Photocopy one sheet for each two photographs you will be using. Trim as necessary and mount the photographs on the photocopied seed packets with glue. Make the required number of colour photocopies of each sheet.

LEFT: *The front of the packet needs no labelling. On the reverse, write the name of the plant, the date and cultivation instructions.*

3 Cut the packet out using scissors or a craft knife and metal ruler.

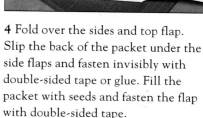

4 Fold over the sides and top flap. Slip the back of the packet under the side flaps and fasten invisibly with double-sided tape or glue. Fill the packet with seeds and fasten the flap with double-sided tape.

DECOUPAGE SEED STORAGE BOX

· · ❧ · ·

Some seeds will still germinate after thousands of years, while others have a far briefer span in which they remain capable of germination. Nowadays, seeds come with a "use by" date printed on the packet and, where indicated, the seeds can be saved for use the next year. Thrown into an empty pot in the corner of the shed, they may just survive attack by damp and insects, but a far better bet is to store them in a tin or box with a snugly fitting lid. This simple decoupage technique, using photocopied engravings of fruit and vegetables, turns an ordinary box into a decorative gift.

Materials and Equipment
PVA glue and wallpaper paste
paintbrushes
photocopies of fruit and vegetable
engravings
craft knife or small scissors
cutting mat or thick card
box or tin
water-based matt varnish
artist's raw umber acrylic paint
crackle glaze (optional)

1 Dilute one part PVA glue with two parts water and brush over the photocopied sheets to "set" the ink and ensure that the paper does not stretch. Leave to dry.

2 Cut round the images with the craft knife, protecting the work surface with a cutting mat or thick card. Alternatively the images can be cut out using a small pair of very sharp, pointed scissors.

3 Mix up a small amount of wallpaper paste following the manufacturer's instructions. Brush paste on to the back of the images. Position the images on the lid and sides of the box. As the paste dries slowly, you may reposition as necessary.

4 When the paste is fully dry, seal the lid with several coats of water-based matt varnish, allowing each coat to dry completely before applying the next. To give the box an aged appearance, add a little raw umber acrylic paint to the varnish and mix well. To create an even more antiqued effect, the box may be finished with a crackle glaze (available from good art shops).

LEFT: Isolated areas of the images can be hand-tinted with watercolour paint, this needs to be done before the PVA glue is applied.

ROW MARKERS

· · ❧ · ·

In early spring, when the vegetable garden is little more than a patch of bare soil with seeds secretly germinating out of sight, there is a risk of losing track of just what has been planted where. Ordinary labels used as row markers can be kicked over, misplaced when pulled out to read what is written on them or even pulled up by birds. These unusual large-scale row markers are both decorative and functional. Anyone who uses them will be in no doubt about where they planted their vegetables and will be able to read what has been planted and when, without kneeling down in the damp spring soil.

Materials and Equipment
wooden broom handles
ruler
saw
fine-grade sandpaper
wooden knobs, 4 cm (1 1/2 in) in
diameter
PVA glue
matt woodwash or emulsion paint
paintbrush
metal plant labels
gold marker pen
garden string
drill (optional)

2 Paint the row marker with one or two coats of matt woodwash or emulsion paint. Leave to dry.

1 For each row marker, cut a 70 cm (28 in) length of a wooden broom handle. Check that the cut is straight and rub down the sawn edge with fine-grade sandpaper until it is smooth. Attach a wooden knob using PVA glue. Leave it all to dry overnight, or until the glue is fully hardened.

3 Brush a coat of matching woodwash or paint on to the metal plant label. Leave to dry, then rub down lightly with fine-grade sandpaper for a distressed look.

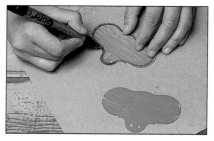

4 Carefully outline the label with a gold marker pen. Attach the label to the row marker. You can do this either by tying garden string around the knob or by drilling a hole through the marker just below the knob, threading the garden string through and knotting it securely.

LEFT: Small terracotta pots on canes can be used as appealing row markers that double up as earwig catchers.

VEGETABLE SACKS

· · ❧ · ·

Hessian sacks are ideal for storing root vegetables in good condition in a potting shed or out-house, especially when they are hung on hooks so that the air can circulate freely and mice can be kept at bay. Fringed calico squares decorated with homely stencilled vegetable motifs have been stitched on to these sacks to make them decorative and functional. Make them for a keen vegetable grower, or fill them with your own produce as a gift. The idea can be adapted to make attractive garden cushions.

Materials and Equipment
tracing paper
pencil
stencil card
aerosol glue
stencil knife
cutting mat or newspaper
acrylic or fabric paints
stencil brush
calico, 20 x 25 cm (8 x 10 in), with
edges fringed
scrap paper or kitchen roll
hessian, 40 x 120 cm (16 x 48 in)
dressmaker's pins
sewing machine or needle
matching cotton thread

1 Enlarge and trace the vegetable stencil templates from the back of the book onto tracing paper. Stick the tracing paper to the stencil card with aerosol glue.

RIGHT: *Stencilled motifs immediately identify the contents of the sacks.*

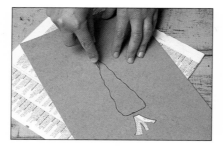

2 Cut out the design with a stencil knife, protecting the work surface with a cutting mat or newspaper.

3 Prepare your paints and stencil the design on to the calico using a stippling action. The stencil brush should be as dry as possible for successful stencilling, so have a piece of scrap paper or kitchen roll handy to wipe any excess paint off the brush before you begin.

4 Apply more paint in a stippling motion to one side of the carrot, onion and potato for a rounded, three-dimensional effect. Leave the paint to dry.

RIGHT: *Store home-grown vegetables carefully to last through the winter.*

5 Fold the hessian in half, so that it measures 40 x 60 cm (16 x 24 in). Position the stencilled panel on the front of the hessian and pin in place so that it is neatly centred.

6 Stitch the panel in place and then make up the sack. Finish all raw edges with double seams or zigzag stitch to prevent fraying.

WEATHERED GARDEN FURNITURE
· · ~ · ·

Simple folding chairs, once used in their thousands in municipal parks, are now desirable objects with their faded paintwork and weathered wood, and they fetch premium prices. A far less expensive alternative is to buy hardwood folding chairs from a DIY store and do a bit of instant weathering yourself. Waxing the sanded wood before painting, then rubbing down with wire wool, simulates years of wear. When the chair is left out in the garden, nature will continue the process.

2 Rub over the surface randomly with the candle, applying the wax thickly on the corners and edges.

3 Paint the chair with white emulsion paint using random brush strokes and leave to dry completely.

4 Rub down with the wire wool to remove paint from the waxed areas.

ABOVE: *A similar technique was applied to this wheelbarrow, which is being used to display trugs of violas.*

Materials and Equipment
folding wooden garden chair
medium-grade sandpaper
household candle
one-coat white emulsion paint
paintbrush
wire wool

1 Rub down the surface of the chair with sandpaper to make a better key for the paint.

CUSTOMIZED NESTING BOX

· · ⟡ · ·

A simple, inexpensive birdhouse can be transformed into a charming garden detail with a lick of paint and a few decorative touches. The Shaker-style paintwork uses leftover paint, the finial is cut from scrap timber and the perch is a small apple twig. If you think your birds might prefer a more metropolitan dwelling, paint the nesting box blue-grey and roof it with some copper foil. Use a scrap of copper foil to make a door surround, ensuring that no sharp edges are left which might injure the birds. If the nesting box is hung so that it can be seen from the house it will give maximum pleasure.

Materials and Equipment
nesting box
emulsion paint in 2 colours
paintbrush
permanent marker pen
decorative finial cut from a piece of
scrap pine
PVA glue
drill
apple twig

3 Fill in the design and the finial with the second colour of emulsion paint and leave to dry completely.

4 Glue the finial in place at the front of the roof ridge using PVA glue.

5 Drill a hole of the same diameter as the apple twig beneath the entrance hole. Apply a little glue to the twig and push it in position.

1 Paint the box with the first colour of emulsion paint and leave to dry.

2 Draw the door and heart motifs with the permanent marker pen.

LEFT: Birds will be more likely to use the nesting boxes if they are hung well out of reach of cats and other predators and in a position where overhanging foliage will provide them with some shelter and a little privacy.

WIND CHIMES

· · ❧ · ·

A walk on the beach or in the woods to gather weathered twigs and a forage around the potting shed will provide you with all the materials for these rustic wind chimes. The bells are made from miniature terracotta pots with metal vine-eyes as clappers.

Provided the pots have no cracks, the wind chimes will sound like distant cow-bells to add a third sensual dimension to the visual and fragrant delights of summer. They make a perfect finishing touch to an informal country garden.

Materials and Equipment
110 cm (44 in) galvanized wire
wire cutters
4 weathered twigs of different sizes,
the largest 30 cm (12 in) long
drill
3 corks
2 vine-eyes
5 cm (2 in) old terracotta pots

1 Cut the wire into one 50 cm (20 in) length and two 30 cm (12 in) lengths using wire cutters. Make a hanging loop at one end of the 50 cm (20 in) length.

2 Twist the wire around the centre of the longest twig. Drill a hole through the centre of each of the corks and thread one on to the wire.

3 Add the next twig, either by twisting the wire around it as before, or by drilling a hole through the centre and threading it on.

4 Add a second cork to the wire, followed by the third twig attached as before and the third cork.

ABOVE: *Alternative materials for wind chimes could include shells and sand dollars threaded with raffia.*

5 Make a hook from the remaining length of wire and trim if necessary. Drill a hole through one end of the final twig and hook it on to the wire.

6 Thread a vine-eye on to each of the two 30 cm (12 in) lengths of wire and bend over 2.5 cm (1 in) of the wire so that it lies flat against the vine-eye. Wrap the other end of the wire around the vine-eye in a spiral.

7 Thread each vine-eye through the hole in one of the terracotta pots, so that the wide end of the vine-eye becomes the clapper. Hang up the wind chimes, making sure that they balance, and twist the wires protruding from the bells securely around the ends of the first twig.

NATURAL
GARDEN GIFTS

· · ❦ · ·

*Stunning ideas for presenting flowers and herbs from
the garden, from posies and elegant topiaries to
symbolic gifts hidden in the meaning of flowers.*

TRIBUTE TO MONET
· · 🙦 · ·

Anyone fortunate enough to have visited Monet's beautiful house and garden at Giverny will appreciate the vivid colours to be seen in both and is bound to have been influenced by his vision. One of his favourite combinations of colour was blue and yellow, and this project uses both these colours to decorate a simple wire basket. The basket is then lined with moss and planted with coloured pansies in a tribute to the great artist's glorious palette and his passionate love of gardening and gardens.

Materials and Equipment
wooden-handled wire basket
masking tape
blue car-spray paint
large cardboard box
yellow woodstain
paintbrush
moss
3 pansy plants
compost

1 Mask the handle of the basket with masking tape and spray the basket blue. It is better to apply two or three thin coats than one thick one, as the paint has a tendency to run if applied too thickly. Leave to dry between applications. Use the spray paint in a well-ventilated area and place the basket in a large cardboard box, lying on its side, to limit the spread of the fine droplets of paint. Avoid inhaling the fumes. Leave to dry completely.

2 Remove the masking tape from the handle and paint it with the yellow woodstain. Leave to dry, then add further coats for a more intense colour. Allow to dry completely.

3 Line the basket with moss and, removing the pansies from their pots, plant them in the basket. Fill around the plants with extra compost if necessary and then tuck more moss around them. Water well and leave the basket to drain.

LEFT: *Choose pansies in a rich, velvety shade of red to complement the clear fresh blue and yellow of the basket.*

TOPIARY HERBS

· · ⁕ · ·

This is one of the most attractive and stylish ways of growing herbs, especially when they are planted in "long tom" pots, which complete the sculptural effect. The herbs suitable for this treatment are those with woody stems such as rosemary, lemon verbena, santolina and lavender. Select young plants with a strong, straight central stem, which can be trimmed to create the topiary shape. Topiary herbs are attractive as centrepieces for a paved herb garden, and they make elegant gifts. They will need to be pruned every two weeks during the growing season, to keep them in good shape.

Materials and Equipment
scissors
young herb plants: rosemary,
lavender, santolina or lemon verbena
selection of terracotta pots, ideally
"long toms"
compost
coarse grit
washed gravel

ABOVE: *Aromatic lavender is popular both for its beauty and culinary uses.*

LEFT: *The dramatic shape of the topiary is best seen against a plain background.*

1 Using the scissors, trim any side shoots from the central stem of each plant and remove the foliage from the bottom two-thirds of the stem.

2 Trim the remaining foliage to a pleasing, symmetrical shape.

3 Transplant the herb into a terracotta pot using a mixture of two parts compost to one part coarse grit. Plant firmly, first gently loosening the herb's root ball to ensure that the roots quickly settle into the new compost.

4 Cover the top layer of compost with a layer of washed gravel. Water well and stand in a sheltered, sunny position.

THE LANGUAGE OF FLOWERS

· · 🙝 · ·

There has been a long tradition of attaching meaning to certain flowers which reached its peak when the Victorian leisured classes devised their rather whimsical and arbitrary "language of flowers". In those days, any man wishing to impress a woman who was versed in this language would have to negotiate his way through a minefield of potential dangers, for in some cases it was not simply the variety of flower but also its colour that carried a message. The posy assembled here carries the message, "I sincerely adore and esteem your praiseworthy good taste". Not exactly romantic, but it would be fun to make for someone who has been decorating or just moved house.

Materials and Equipment
sunflowers ("adoration")
fennel ("worthy of praise")
fuchsia ("taste")
single dahlia ("good taste")
sage ("esteem")
fern ("sincerity")
bucket
garden string
50 cm (20 in) ribbon

1 Remove any foliage at the base of the flower stems. Condition the flowers by standing them in deep water in a bucket in a cool place for a couple of hours.

2 Lay out the flowers on a work surface, grouping them by variety.

3 Assemble the posy by adding flowers a few at a time and, holding the posy, rearranging until you are happy with the shape.

4 Tie the stems firmly with string and decorate the posy with ribbon tied in a pretty bow.

LEFT: *Scented pelargonium is a symbol of friendship. Numerous books on the language of flowers were published in the nineteenth century, and some are now available in facsimile.*

LAVENDER BOTTLES

There was a time when nearly every garden grew lavender bushes, and housewives considered harvesting the lavender an essential part of the domestic ritual. Lavender was used in healing and soothing lotions, in flower waters, as a strewing herb and to scent linen. The tradition of scenting linen with lavender originated not in the desire to impart its fragrance to the bedchamber but rather in its considerable insect-repellent properties. The making of lavender bags, sachets and bottles was an essential household task rather than the aromatic pleasure it is today. Much of the lavender that is grown today is the compact form with short flower stems, but if you also grow the taller varieties, you can use them to make lavender bottles. This traditional way of preserving lavender is practical as well as decorative as the stems form a cage around the flower heads, releasing the fragrance but preventing the flowers from dropping. However, a vigorous shake will dislodge some of the flowers and, if you have wooden floors, you can crush a few of the fallen flowers underfoot to fill the room with the scent of lavender.

Materials and Equipment
FOR EACH LAVENDER BOTTLE:
20 fresh lavender stems
string
scissors or secateurs

1 Gather the lavender stems into a neat bundle and tie firmly, but not too tightly, with string just beneath the flower heads. Cut off the loose ends of string.

2 Holding the flower heads in one hand, use the other hand to fold the stems over the flower heads, one at a time. Work systematically until all the stems are folded over the flower heads and the bottle shape is formed.

3 Tie the stems in place about halfway down their length.

4 Trim the ends of the stems level with scissors or secateurs.

LEFT: *Compact varieties of lavender are ideal for making bags and sachets, for which only the flower heads are needed.*

BLOOMING BORAGE

• • ❧ • •

According to the old saying "a garden without borage is a garden without courage", which refers to the belief that this plant has the ability to lift the spirits. Recently, borage has become an important crop as its oils have been found to be as potent as those of evening primrose, and fields of its stunning blue flowers are now a much more common sight. In addition to their medicinal properties, borage flowers floating in a glass of summer punch have the ability to gladden most hearts.

Materials and Equipment
tracing paper
pencil and tape
stencil card
aerosol glue
cutting mat or thick card
stencil knife or craft knife
acrylic paints: mid-blue, deep blue and white
plate
galvanized bucket, 18 cm (7 in) in diameter
stencil brush
paintbrush
borage plant

1 Enlarge and trace the borage flower template from the back of the book on to tracing paper.

2 Mount the tracing on a piece of stencil card using the aerosol glue.

3 Place the stencil card on the cutting mat or thick card and cut out the stencil with a stencil knife or craft knife. Pour some mid-blue paint on to a plate.

5 Use the paintbrush to add details to the flowers in deep blue and white. Place the borage plant in the bucket.

BELOW: The beautiful blue flowers of the borage plant can be used as a salad garnish or to decorate glasses of refreshing summer punch.

4 Stencil the outline of the flowers on to the bucket in a random pattern, overlapping them if you like.

LEFT: A borage plant in a decorated bucket makes a pretty summer gift.

GROW YOUR OWN WINE KIT

· · · ～ *· · ·*

Nothing could be more rewarding than your own grape vines and harvest, and this idea is on the perfect scale for first-time wine-makers to start producing their own *vin de maison*. This kit has been designed as the perfect present for an oenophile friend. A wooden wine-box (in this case, once home to a pleasing vintage of Chateau Lynch-Bages) is varnished for use as an appropriate container and a teasing inspiration to the would-be wine-maker. A suitable variety of grape, available from specialist nurseries, is potted and packed into the box with empty bottles, corks, a demijohn and wine labels.

Materials and Equipment
wooden wine-box
medium-grade sandpaper
varnish
paintbrush
grape vine
terracotta pot
compost
tracing paper
vine leaf
black pen
photocopier
green paper
cutting mat or thick card
stencil knife or craft knife
bark
clean, empty wine bottles, labels removed
new corks
demijohn

RIGHT: A variation on this gift might include a basket of plums and recipes for making fruit spirits.

1 Rub down any rough edges on the wooden box with sandpaper. Seal the box with varnish and leave to dry.

2 Plant the grape vine in the terracotta pot, using extra compost as necessary. Take care not to disturb the roots and remember to water the vine to remove any air that may have gathered around the roots in the compost.

3 To make the labels for the vine and wine-making equipment, place the tracing paper on top of the vine leaf and carefully trace around the edge of the leaf with a black pen. Draw in some of the main veins on the leaf.

4 Photocopy the leaf tracing on green paper to make the required number of labels for the gift.

5 Place the photocopies on the cutting mat or thick card and cut round the leaf shapes with a stencil knife or craft knife.

6 Attach one of the labels to the vine with its name and growing instructions. Fill the box with bark and arrange the components attractively, make sure you include some corks.

BELOW: Bottles and a demijohn are included in the beginner's set.

BOUQUET GARNI

There is a world of difference between fresh or home-dried bouquet garni and the little sachets which sit at the back of most herb racks, slowly losing all resemblance to the fresh herbs from which they were made. The classic bouquet garni consists of parsley, thyme and a bay leaf tied into a posy with string and used to impart flavour to stews, soups and sauces. In all but the coldest areas, it is possible to gather these herbs fresh for the majority of the year, but a small stock of dried bouquet garni, each encased in a little muslin bag, is a good insurance policy against the bleak mid-winter.

Materials and Equipment
drill
wooden crate, approximately
25 x 20 x 15 cm (10 x 8 x 6 in)
40 cm (16 in) sisal rope
permanent marker pen
liquid seaweed plant food
paintbrush
moss
small bay tree
thyme
2 parsley plants
compost
coarse grit

1 Drill two holes in each end of the crate. Thread 20 cm (8 in) of rope through the holes and knot the ends.

2 Use the permanent marker pen to write on each side of the crate.

3 To give the crate a weathered appearance, paint it with a mixture of one part seaweed plant food and one part water. You can make the mixture more or less dilute depending on the finish required.

4 Line the crate with moss.

5 Plant the herbs, using a mixture of three parts compost to one part coarse grit. Press in the plants firmly and tuck more moss around. Water thoroughly.

LEFT: *A bouquet garni – bay, thyme and parsley bound with twine. In Provence rosemary is always added and makes the world of difference to the taste of a stew.*

SAGE AND TANSY HEART

· · ❧ · ·

Like many other herbs, tansy and sage both dry well and are perfect companions. When picked at its prime, tansy will dry maintaining the yellow colouring of the flowers. For this project, a heart shape is formed out of thick wire and small bunches of the herbs are wired in place to make a charming and aromatic decorative hanging that will keep for many years.

Materials and Equipment
pliers
thick, plastic-coated garden wire
fine green florist's wire
30 small bunches of dried sage
12 small bunches of dried tansy
50 cm (20 in) yellow cord

1 Using the pliers, make a small loop at the end of the thick wire. Lay the wire on the work surface and form a circle approximately 30 cm (12 in) in diameter. Repeat to make three more rings of wire lying on top of the first circle. Cut off the wire.

2 Twist the top circle of wire around the others to hold them together.

3 Holding the wire circle firmly in both hands with the loop positioned opposite you, carefully bend into a symmetrical heart shape.

4 Use the fine green florist's wire to bind the small bunches of herbs neatly and securely.

5 Starting at the top of the heart, wire the bunches of herbs on to the frame. Begin with the sage and intersperse each two bunches of sage with one bunch of tansy. Work to the bottom of the heart, then start at the top again to complete the other side.

6 To hang the heart, thread the cord through the loop at the top of the heart and tie in a knot.

LEFT: *The gentle pale green of dried sage leaves is perfectly complemented by bunches of pretty yellow tansy flowers.*

TEMPLATES

· · ✦ · ·

All the templates below are reproduced at a reduced size, so they will need to be enlarged before use. This can be done using a photocopier, or by using a grid system. To do this, draw a grid of evenly spaced squares over the template. On a second sheet of paper, draw a grid with squares twice the size of the previous ones and copy the design, square by square, on to the second grid. Draw over the lines to make sure they are continuous. To transfer the design, use a soft pencil to rub over the back of the new tracing, then right side up, draw over the traced lines with a hard pencil on to the new surface.

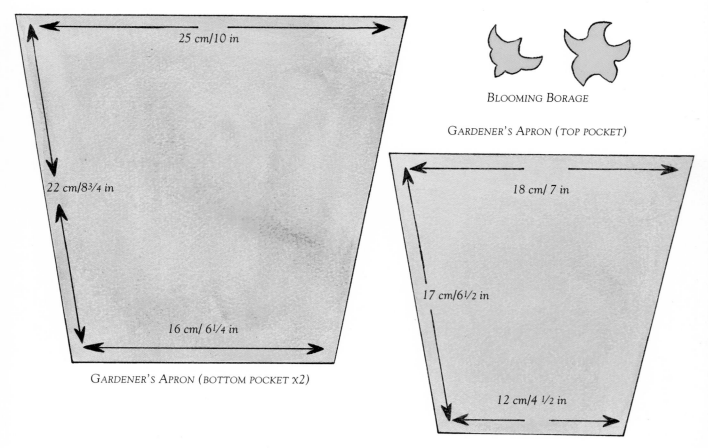

25 cm/10 in

22 cm/8³/4 in

16 cm/ 6¹/4 in

GARDENER'S APRON (BOTTOM POCKET x2)

BLOOMING BORAGE

GARDENER'S APRON (TOP POCKET)

18 cm/ 7 in

17 cm/6¹/2 in

12 cm/4 ¹/2 in

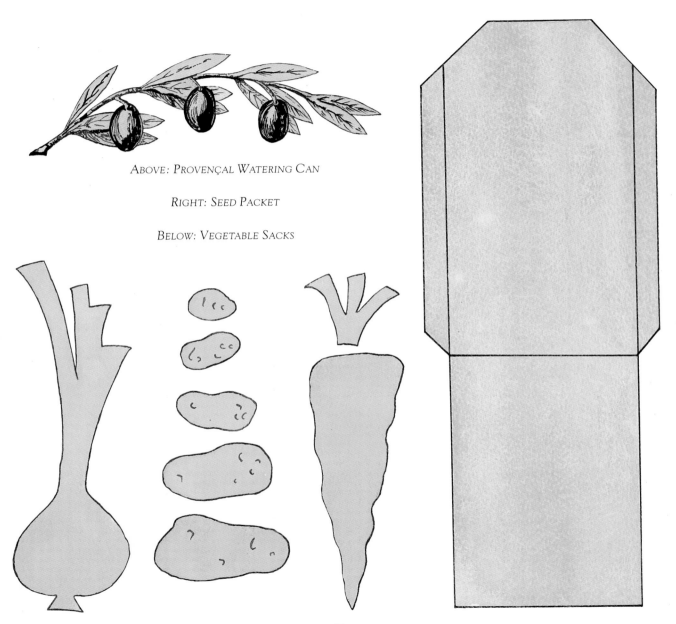

ABOVE: PROVENÇAL WATERING CAN

RIGHT: SEED PACKET

BELOW: VEGETABLE SACKS

INDEX

· · ❧ · ·

A
apron 14–15

B
barrier cream 12
basket, wire 46–7
bay 58
birds, nesting box 40–1
borage, blooming 54–5
bouquet garni 58–9
boxes
  bulbs 28
  nesting 40–1
  seed 32–3
  storage 24–5
  wine kit 56–7
bulbs 28–9

C
chair 38-9
clothing
  scarf 16–17
  Wellington boots 18–19
culinary herbs 58–9
customized nesting box 40–1

D
dahlias 50–1
decorated hand tools 20–1
decorated rubber boots 18–19
decoupage, hand tools 20–1

decoupage, seed storage box
  32–3
decoupage, watering can 22–3
dibber 10

F
fennel 50–1
fern 50–1
flowerpot pockets 14–15
flowers
  language of 50–1
  lavender bottles 52–3
  topiary herbs 48-9
  tribute to Monet 46–7
fork 10
fruit wine kits 56–7
fuchsia 50–1
furniture, garden 38–9

G
garden furniture, weathered
  38–9
gardener's storage box 24–5
gift set 10–11
gloves 10
grape vines, wine kit 56–7

H
hand tools, decorated 20–1
hand-care kit 12–13
heart, sage and tansy 60–1
herald of spring 28–9
herbs
  bay 58
  borage 54–5
  bouquet garni 58–9
  lavender bottles 52–3
  sage and tansy heart 60–1
  topiary 48–9
hessian vegetable sacks 36–7

I
Insect repellent 16

L
labels 10
  row markers 34–5
language of flowers 50–1
lavender 48
  bottles 52–3
lemon oil 12
lemon verbena 48

M
Monet, tribute to 46–7

N
nesting box 40–1
new gardener's gift set 10–11

P
packets, seed 30–1
pansy 46
parsley 58
posies 50–1
Provençal watering can
  22–3

R
rosemary 48
row markers 34–5
rubber boots 18–19

S
sacks
  bulb 28–9
  vegetable 36–7
sage 50
  and tansy heart 60–1
santolina 48
scarf 16–17
secateurs 10
seeds
  packets 30–1
  storage box 32–3
skin care 12–13
spring bulbs 28–9
storage
  boxes 24–5, 32–3
  bulb sacks 28–9
  seed packets 30–1
  vegetable sacks 36–7

T
tansy 60
templates 62–3
thyme 58
topiary herbs 48–9
tribute to Monet 46–7
trowel 10
  decorated 20–1

V
vegetable sacks 36–7

W
watering can, Provençal 22–3
weathered garden furniture
  38–9
weed lifter 10
wheelbarrow 38
wind chimes 42–3
wine kit 56–7